Fostering a Pluralistic Society
Through Multi-Ethnic Education

By Ricardo L. Garcia

Library of Congress Catalog Card Number: 78-50372
ISBN 0-87367-107-4
Copyright© 1978 by The Phi Delta Kappa Educational Foundation
Bloomington, Indiana

81676

TABLE OF CONTENTS

A Test in Current Events

Linda Redcloud returned to her classroom after an active recess. She and her best friend, Sandi, had just finished a vigorous round of T-ball. Linda's teacher was preparing the class for the weekly test in current events.

"Now, boys and girls," he began, "it's time to settle down. Go to your tables, pull out some paper, and answer the questions as I read them." The class quieted down. Midway through the test, he noticed Linda whispering.

"All right, Linda! No talking during exams! Next time I catch you cheating, I'll take your test." He continued the questions. Then,

"Linda, what's in that note you're passing to Sandi?"

"Answers to the questions."

"What! You've got to be kidding! You're not supposed to cheat."

"But, I'm," sputtered Linda, "I'm not cheating. Sandi doesn't know the answers and I'm . . ."

"Yeah, sure, you're helping Sandi." He threw Linda's test paper in the wastebasket.

Was Linda cheating? The facts indicate that she was. Or, do they? What about the facts that Linda, a Seminole native American, was reared in an extended family, consisting of grandparents, parents, and six brothers and sisters? Her parents taught her, above all, to share her things with others in the family and to put the needs of the family above her own. Excessive competition and selfishness for personal gain have no place in her family.

Almost daily, many students in American public schools experience assaults like this on their ethnic values. Quietly, they adjust to these assaults, conceal their beliefs, and suppress their feelings. They learn to cope, to tune in or tune out as the occasion demands. The cultural conflict students confront in schools is fundamentally one of misunderstanding. Teachers do not understand ethnicity. Teachers neither know, nor have they been taught, that ethnicity, racism, and ethnocentrism are endemic factors in American society that influence teaching and learning. Much of the cultural conflict is not so much a case of the "redneck teacher bent on suppressing minorities" as it is a case of teachers who have not been prepared to teach ethnically different students. With minor exceptions, colleges of education have abdicated their responsibility to prepare teachers to understand the cultural milieu from which students emerge.

Educational history and sociology are generally included in teacher preparation programs. These courses usually survey 200 years of American education, but such critical issues as industrialization, assimilation, mass education, segregation, desegregation, and integration are treated superficially. Teachers cannot be expected to learn about ethnicity by consuming knowledge in sociology or history of education courses. Teachers must be directed to experience ethnicity—their own as well as the students'—through field experiences in classroom settings where they interact with students on a daily basis and deal firsthand with educational concerns involving ethnicity.

The gap in teacher education—ethnic and cultural education—results from assimilation policies promulgated in the early part of the twentieth century. To assimilate immigrant students into Anglo-American culture, schools instituted Americanization programs to wean immigrant students from their native languages and cultures and replace them with the American English language and Anglo culture. Manifestations of ethnicity were discouraged. Non-Christian observances, foreign languages, and native costumes were perceived as "un-American." Melting away ethnic differences was a function of good teaching.

While teachers are no longer trained to melt away ethnic differences, they are seldom encouraged or trained to recognize and utilize

6

these differences as educational tools. The Bicentennial Commission on Education of the American Association of Colleges for Teacher Education (AACTE) reports that "teachers are not prepared either personally or professionally for such services. Most have been reared in middle- or lower middle-class homes and communities, ensconced safely away from the concentrations of minority and lower socioeconomic groups. Many possess a conventional wisdom bias toward minorities." During the past decade, teachers were taught that minority students were culturally deprived, and, thereby, disadvantaged. The theories of disadvantage described minority group cultures as deficient. Purportedly, these dysfunctional cultures did not provide minority youth with the skills and knowledge necessary for school success. The culture-of-poverty theory postulated that minority group cultures were dysfunctional because impoverished parents nurtured anti-learning attitudes among the youth.

We now know that minority students cannot be culturally deprived. Minority groups have functional cultures that are assimilated by their youth. Minority group members are found in most socioeconomic classes. However, what minority group parents feel their youth should learn often differs from what teachers expect them to learn. Minority students are disadvantaged to the extent that their cultures differ from the dominant culture of the school. Thus, cultural conflict in the classroom is subtle and unconscious, sometimes unrecognized by the teacher. In the case of Linda Redcloud, was it so wrong for her to share answers? Should the teacher be expected to know that for Linda sharing answers to an exam is no different from sharing food or clothing? Was the teacher correct, or incorrect, to infer that Linda cheated? Indeed, who failed the test in current events? Linda or the teacher?

Answering these questions is not easy. Teaching is an exceedingly complex task. Everything about teaching is in a constant state of flux. Students, social conditions, and instructional materials change. Parents, school boards, administrators, professional education organizations, teacher educators, and civic groups flood the teacher with differing perspectives on the nature of students, learning, teaching, and the good life. Multi-ethnic education complicates teaching even further by adding ethnicity as a basic factor in teaching.

Ethnicity encompasses the cultural orientations of students, teachers, and other school personnel. It refers to the feelings, perceptions, attitudes, beliefs, and physical characteristics associated with ethnic group membership. It affects one's sense of time and space and refers to a sense of belonging to an ethnic group. Transmitting culture and socializing youth are basic goals of the public school. Multi-ethnic education extends these social goals because it is intended for *all* students in *all* schools. It is not a euphemism for "education of the disadvantaged."

The purpose of multi-ethnic education is to prepare students to live harmoniously in a multi-ethnic society by 1) reflecting in school curricula the ethnic diversity of American society, 2) dealing directly with ethnic group similarities and differences, and 3) providing students with experiences and opportunities to understand their uniqueness in a pluralistic milieu. *The anticipated outcomes of multi-ethnic education are dissipation of racism, ethnocentrism, group prejudices, and intergroup conflicts, with concurrent enhancement of human empathy, dignity, and respect. There is nothing new about championing the causes of student integrity, human respect, and social harmony. Multi-ethnic education is designed to champion these causes for all students, including ethnic minorities whose cultures and languages have been excluded or disparaged in school curricula.*

Ethnic Groups and Ethnicity

An ethnic group is a unique type of human group. Definitions of an ethnic group range from "the ground we stand on" to an "interest group" held together by language loyalty and cultural ties. Some social scientists believe an ethnic group must also have a "sense of peoplehood," or a feeling of cohesion based on common experiences and fates. For example, Mexican Americans call their group *La Raza*, to connote "the people." The term implies a sense of peoplehood, a feeling of belonging and identifying with the Mexican American group.

A universal human trait is to form groups centered on common interests, needs, and aspirations. The group develops patterns of behavior, systems of belief, communication networks, and a technology to promote survival. Established patterns become traditions; established beliefs become *ethos* or *mores*. *Ethos* are the group's commonly held values, and *mores* are the group's taboos, norms, or moral restrictions.

Ethos and mores control individual behavior by prescribing social parameters and constraints that force the individual to conform. In a democracy the group does not insist on total conformity, because total conformity would stifle creativity, innovation, and change. The group must tolerate a certain amount of deviance to survive. This principle of tolerable deviation allows group heterogeneity, intragroup diversity, and individual development. It also prevents oppressive conformity, uniform thinking, and suppression of individuality. The principle allows diversity, and while it prescribes normative parameters, it prevents the suffocating group conformity imposed by totalitarian ideologies such as those portrayed in Aldous Huxley's *Brave New World* or George Orwell's *1984*.

9

For example, within their ethnic group Mexican Americans are bound together by a common language, Spanish; Roman Catholic moral precepts; liberal political doctrines (influenced by Mexican socialism); and deeply felt family ties. Individually, Mexican Americans differ vastly. Not all speak or think in Spanish. Some use English only. Others speak various dialects of Spanish. Not all are Roman Catholics. Some are Protestants of evangelical sects; not all are liberals. Many are conservative Democrats; others are progressive Republicans. Others belong to splinter parties, such as the Chicano party, *La Raza Unida*. Not all have strong family ties. Some have nuclear families; others have extended families including grandparents, *compadres* (godparents), and third generation grandchildren.

The group transmits culture through institutions. In preindustrial societies the young were socialized by the family to live within the group. Socialization began at birth and extended beyond puberty. At puberty the individual was inducted into tne adult group via some rite of passage. Parents socialized their children by teaching them the ethnic group's ethos, mores, traditions, and technical skills. Education of youth was the family's essential function and the parents' primary responsibility.

In contemporary society the family has delegated educational responsibilities to other institutions. Now education of youth is shared with the church and school. Teachers and others serve *in loco parentis* and thus share in our youth's technical and spiritual education. Cultural conflict is likely to occur in the schools when the teacher's and the ethnic group's socialization practices differ.

We cannot ignore ethnicity, for it is a cultural heritage consisting of blends of religious, racial, national, and social influences. For some ethnic groups, such as Jews, religious and political status are key influences. For others, such as blacks and Asians, racial characteristics and social status are key influences. For transnational groups, economic, racial, and regional status are key influences. Some Americans can trace their ethnic heritage to several nations and hence identify as members of transnational ethnic groups; some members of transnational groups are not sure they have an ethnic group. Or they may not consciously affiliate with an ethnic group. Many will say they have no

10

ethnic group and that they are a "Heinz 57" variety, i.e., of mixed national origins.

A person's ethnic group in American society is not synonymous with his language or nationality. In nineteenth-century Europe a person's ethnic group was also his nationality. Many times his ethnic, national, and language group were the same. A Spaniard (ethnic group) was Spanish (nationality) and spoke Spanish (language group). Citizens of the U.S. call themselves Americans and perceive their national allegiance to be to the United States of America. One can have an American nationality, a particular ethnic group, e.g., Greek American, and speak an American variety of the English language.

There are four large ethnic minority groups in American society: Asian Americans, black Americans, native Americans, and Spanish-speaking Americans. The 1,000,000 Asian Americans consist of Chinese, Japanese, Filipinos, Koreans, and other Asiatics; the 22,000,000 black Americans comprise the largest racial minority group; the 1,000,000 native Americans represent a multitude of tribes with different languages, including native Hawaiians, Eskimos, and other indigenous groups in American territories; the 9,000,000 Spanish-speaking Americans consist of Mexican Americans, Puerto Ricans, Cubans, and other Latinos. This is the largest bilingual minority group in the U.S.

These groups are identified as minority groups because their members do not control the political or economic institutions that govern or regulate their lives, and their members have retained non-Anglo cultural and linguistic attributes. Traditionally, these groups have been oppressed by laws, customs, folkways, and other social forces that undermine each group's unique status in American society. Although individual group members may not personally feel oppressed, it is a historical fact that ethnic groups have been subjugated.

Ethnic minority groups and poverty groups are not synonymous. While many ethnic minority people are poor, poverty is not a condition inherent to ethnic minority groups. Each has a wide spectrum of membership in most social classes; poverty is a condition experienced by most ethnic groups, but minority groups have no monopoly on poverty.

11

Struggles Between Ideals and Realities

The dominant ethnic group in American society is made up of much-maligned white, Anglo-Saxon, Protestants (WASPs). The power of our WASP heritage is still potent, manifested in major institutions, in people's attitudes and behaviors. The WASP group is so deeply embedded in American society that its attitudes and values are perceived by some to be *the* American core ethos.

I use the WASP acronym to describe and not to disparage this dominant ethnic group. The acronym has come to have negative connotations such as bigot and "redneck." The implications are clearly unfair and grossly incorrect, because bigotry, hypocrisy, and other human vexations are not characteristic of any one group. Actually, WASPs make up a majority ethnic group because of their political and economic power, and the acronym accurately identifies their ethnic heritage, cultural orientations, and religious influences.

The core ethos or commonly shared value system of American society consists of universal ethical precepts, moral admonitions, and natural rights included in such documents as the Declaration of Independence, U.S. Constitution, Mosaic Law, Gettysburg Address, and the "I Have a Dream" speech by Martin Luther King, Jr. King said,

> I still have a dream. It is a dream deeply rooted in the American Dream. I have a dream that one day this nation will rise up and live out the true meaning of its creed. . . . I have a dream that my children will one day live in a nation where they will not be judged by the color of their skins but by the contents of their character.

WASP values and common core values have frequently been in

conflict. The core values presume the equality of all individuals regardless of color or creed—"they will not be judged by the color of their skins"—while WASP values presume the superiority of the white race, Anglo-Saxon institutions, and the Protestant ethic of individualism and self-reliance. Madison Grant's treatise, *The Passing of the Great Race*, embodied the notion of white racial superiority:

> Whether we like to admit it or not, the result of the mixture of two races, in the long run, gives us a race reverting to the more ancient, generalized, and lower type. The cross between a white man and an Indian is an Indian; the cross between a white man and a Negro is a Negro.

Every ethnic group has its myths. Myths synthesize the group's ideals and ethos. Each group struggles to reconcile its realities with its ideals. In American life we have struggled to reconcile the realities of domination of WASP values with the ideals of our core ethos. White race superiority and ethnic minority inferiority—as genetically determined traits—arose as functional myths to perpetuate WASP domination of American society.

An American Dilemma, Gunnar Myrdal's study of blacks and other minorities in American society, identified America's dilemma as a conflict in doctrines. Myrdal observed that "Americans of all origins have something in common, a social ethos, a political creed, the American creed [that] cements the structure." He spoke of the American creed as the equality principle that conflicted with the "anti-amalgamation doctrine;" which expounded that minorities—blacks and Asians especially—were unmeltable into American, white society due to genetic and cultural inferiority. Myrdal noted that "this attitude of refusing to consider amalgamation—felt and expressed in the entire country—constitutes the center in the complex of attitudes, the common denominator in the problem." The doctrine split the nation into two racial groups, white and colored, neutralized the American creed, and inhibited its application.

The superiority-inferiority myths were rationalized by a vaguely explicated racial and genetic typology. According to the typology, there were two human races, the white race and the colored race, which were arranged in hierarchical order within the WASP melting pot (see Figure 1).

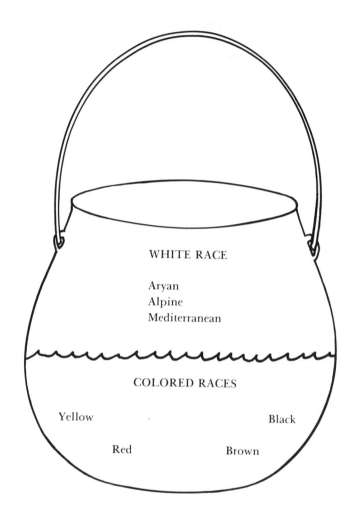

FIGURE I

White/Colored Races in WASP Melting Pot

Within the white race hierarchy, the Nordic or Aryan strain was the superior, pure strain. It consisted of the older German and English immigration stock of ostensibly tall, blond, blue-eyed people. The Alpine strain was less pure; it consisted of darker, eastern European immigrants who were the in-between strain. The lowest white strain was the Mediterranean, which consisted of the dark-haired southern Europeans. In 1909, education historian Ellwood Cubberly expressed the genetic thesis in *Changing Conceptions of Education:* "These southern and eastern Europeans are of a different type from the northern Europeans who preceded them. Illiterate, docile, lacking in self-reliance and initiative, and not possessing the Anglo-Tuetonic conception of law, order, and government, their coming has served to dilute tremendously our national stock. . . . "

Members of the yellow races (Chinese, Japanese, etc.), the red race (native Americans), the brown races (Latinos, Mexican Americans, Hispanics), and the black race were considered unmeltable into the white culture. The colored race, or the "people of color," was unmeltable and would stick to the bottom of the pot. Even the great advocate of world peace and international rapprochement, Woodrow Wilson, expressed his belief in the unmeltability of ethnic minorities when he proclaimed in a 1914 California speech that "the whole question is one of assimilation of diverse races. We cannot make a homogeneous population of a people who do not blend with the Caucasian race." More than 100,000 copies of this position statement were distributed in California.

Laws were passed and traditions formed to prevent minorities from full assimilation into white culture. Studies on exogamy show that a relatively small number of interethnic or interracial marriages occur. Many would-be interracial and interethnic marriages are discouraged with specious rationalizations about social class or religious incompatibility when the objections are really about the person's ethnic or racial group affiliation. Rarely does a minority male marry a white female. Social pressures, especially the notion that the female would be marrying below her group, have successfully controlled mixed marriages even when the potential spouse was reared by parents whose profession or wealth should ascribe them equal social status.

Henry Steele Commager characterized American racism as lawlessness under which a conscious effort is made to maintain second-class citizenship for ethnic minorities. In his *Growth of the American Republic*, co-authored by Samuel Eliot Morison, ethnic minorities were described as people "who were herded into ghettoes, segregated in most public places, fobbed off with inferior schooling, cold-shouldered by labor unions, and assigned to the most menial jobs." The authors described ethnic minority segregation as a volatile American issue that would some day erupt.

In the middle sixties the ghettos exploded. "Burn, baby, burn" was the rallying cry as blacks incinerated the urban symbols of their conquerors, the slum tenement houses; Chicanos rioted against barrio conditions; urban native Americans protested police harassment. In 1967 the Kerner *Report to the National Advisory Commission on Civil Disorders* concluded that the causes of black urban disorders were directly attributable to an endemic illness in American society. "White racism is essentially responsible for the explosive mixture which has accumulated in our cities," the report said.

School Discrimination and Ethnic Minority Students

In 1954 the Supreme Court decision in *Brown* v. *Topeka Board of Education* attempted to eradicate racial discrimination in the public schools. The *Brown* decision quashed the then prevailing "separate but equal" doctrine on the premise that separated, "segregated" school facilities were inherently unequal, that they were psychologically harmful to white and minority students alike, and that they were conduits for the perpetuation of a segregated society. The decision mandated the desegregation of public schools and the ultimate integration of classrooms.

The *Brown* decision emerged as a reconstructionist doctrine that utilizes the school to restructure the social order. *Brown* was expected to impose a more equitable alignment of majority and minority groups. Legal identities of the groups were balanced; the majority group was no longer able to view itself as superior and the minority groups were no longer willing to view their inferior status as the natural social order. With the new alignments, and the consequential new images, fundamental changes in the social order would be possible, changes that would strike at the core of institutionalized racism. The WASP group could no longer rationalize away ethnic minority human and civil rights.

In spite of the sweeping legal mandate of the *Brown* decision, progress toward school desegregation has been painfully slow. Desegregation first encountered violent resistance; later it encountered delaying tactics. Sometimes these maneuvers created the illusion that desegregation had occurred. Yet the Office of Civil Rights reports that, 21 years after *Brown*, less than 40% of all southern schools and about 1% of all northern schools are, in fact, actually desegregated. We still live in a segregated society.

School personnel who deal with ethnic minority students must recognize that desegregation, integration, and multi-ethnic education are components of reconstructionist doctrine designed to counteract the myths of WASP superiority. Note that the results of standardized tests administered over a span of years demonstrate that ethnic minority students begin the primary grades with approximately the same scores as the majority. By the time minority students reach the upper elementary grades, they exhibit a progressive reading deficit in comparison with majority students. Also, attrition rates for minority students are excessive. Two to four times as many black, Mexican American, Puerto Rican, and native American students drop out of high school as do whites; ethnic minority students average two or more years behind national norms in arithmetic and reading; and ethnic minority students get expelled or placed in classes for the mentally retarded more often than do white students.

Achievement and IQ tests have served to perpetuate the myth that WASP students are intellectually superior to ethnic minority students. Studies show that WASP majority students as a group perform better on standardized tests than do ethnic minority students. Using these kinds of data, psychologist Arthur Jensen has argued that white intellectual superiority over blacks is a genetically determined fact. Such arguments ignore the history of discrimination in schools and in American society at large, which reflect the endemic racist attitudes of white superiority.

Educational Exclusion of Blacks

When blacks were kept as slaves, the only education they received was the destruction of their self-respect through servility and obedience. Later, blacks were legally "emancipated" but were economically and socially isolated and excluded by way of legal segregation, Jim Crow laws, and terror. Richard James, in *The Educational Needs of Black Americans*, says, "Although public education in the several states was established by law, white hostility toward the idea of educating blacks persisted. Efforts to provide instruction in an integrated setting were fiercely resisted . . . thwarted by a series of Supreme Court decisions that gave legal respectability to segregation. As a further accommodation to white hostility, the idea of a special kind of education for blacks was proposed. This was industrial education—instruction in agricultural, mechanical, and household industries."

The function of this "special education" was exclusion. The black was educated into roles and occupations that required leadership by the white. This process of maintaining the social order of black inferiority led to the development of black schools and colleges to provide training for blacks in professional as well as vocational occupations.

An intellectual elite developed within the black community, with leadership coming from individuals such as Booker T. Washington, W.E.B. Du Bois, and organizations such as the NAACP (National Association for the Advancement of Colored People). Still, the black remained isolated by racism. It was the 1954 *Brown* decision striking down legal segregation of public facilities and schools that again reminded the WASP group that the "invisible man" would not vanish. Ideally, legal integration would lead to social assimilation of blacks and whites. Instead, a form of one-sided integration evolved—the process of absorbing the black (and other minorities) into WASP schools.

Educational Exclusion of Chicanos

The Chicano experience with American public schools exemplifies ethnic discrimination at its extreme. First, the schools attempted to educate the Chicano by eradicating Chicano language and culture and replacing them with English and Anglo culture. Public schools in the southwest U.S. have as a matter of policy enforced a "no Spanish rule" that prohibits the use of Spanish on school premises. Chicanos have been fined, suspended, and paddled for speaking Spanish in school. As recently as 1970, 69.8% of the schools in the southwest U.S. enforced the rule.

It is now unlawful to enforce the no Spanish rule as a matter of policy. Nevertheless the minimal number of bilingual-bicultural programs in operation has had little impact on the long-standing policies prohibiting Chicano culture and language in the school. Only 3% of the Chicano student population is presently served by such programs, even though the 1973 *Lau* v. *Nichols* Supreme Court decision encourages bilingual programs for non-English-speaking students, and even though federal funds under Title VII of the Elementary and Secondary Education Act (and some state funds) are available for bilingual-bicultural programs.

The schools attempted to educate Chicanos by teaching them English language arts. The attempt failed. By the twelfth grade 63% of the Chicano student population read six months below the national norm, with 24% of these still reading at the ninth-grade level or lower. These Chicanos are the elite 60% who have remained in school after an estimated 40% have dropped out. Only 5.5% of the Chicano students have received some form of instruction in English as a second language. Less than 2% of all teachers of Chicano students are assigned to programs in English as a second language, and most of these teachers have no more than six semester hours in the methodology of this teaching task. Chicano students generally score lower on reading proficiency and verbal achievement tests and participate less in those school activities requiring verbal proficiency.

The schools have tended to exclude the Chicano from meaningful educational experiences. The U.S. Commission on Civil Rights conducted research in southwestern schools involving Chicano and Anglo students to study the verbal interaction among them and their teachers. The study, published under the title *Teachers and Students*, reports that southwestern teachers express a bias against Chicano students by speaking less to Chicanos, praising them less, and asking them fewer questions. "The total picture of classroom interaction . . . is that of a teaching process which is failing to involve the Mexican American student to the same extent as the Anglo pupil, both in terms of quantity and quality of interaction. Teachers speak less often, and less favorably, to Mexican Americans than to Anglos. . . . In view of the central importance of interaction to learning, it is evident that Chicano pupils are not receiving the same quality of education in the classrooms as are Anglo pupils." The study's results indicate that teachers often unconsciously discriminate against Chicano students.

In civil rights legislation, "discrimination" means any direct or indirect act of exclusion, distinction, differentiation, or preference on account of race, religion, color, sex, national origin, or ancestry. The legislation outlaws direct acts of discrimination, such as segregation, as well as indirect acts that have a disproportionate negative effect on ethnic and racial minority students. In 1972 the U.S. Office of Civil Rights investigated discrimination against ethnic minority students. Enrolled in the schools under investigation were 2,414,179 Spanish-surnamed, 232,766 native American, and 233,190 Asian American students. Data were collected on the consistently lower achievement of ethnic minority students and their enrollment in disproportionate numbers of segregated ability-grouped and special education classes. The Office of Civil Rights concluded that ethnic minority students were being excluded from full participation in the educational programs of the school districts investigated.

A policy statement was prepared—the May 25th Memorandum—to protect the right of ethnic minority students to equal educational opportunity. The memorandum—a federal regulation that has the effect of law—specified four areas of educational practices requiring compliance with the Civil Rights Act of 1964:

1. Where inability to speak and understand the English language excludes national origin minority group children from effective participation in the educational program offered by a school district, the district must take affirmative steps to rectify the language deficiency in order to open its instructional program to these students.

2. School districts must not assign national origin minority group students to classes for the mentally retarded on the basis of criteria which essentially measure or evaluate English language skills; nor may school districts deny national origin minority group children access to college preparatory courses on a basis directly related to the failure of the school system to teach English language skills.

3. Any ability-grouping or tracking system employed by the school system to deal with the special language skill needs of national origin minority group children must be designed to meet such language skill needs as soon as possible and must not operate as an educational dead end or permanent track.

4. School districts have the responsibility to adequately notify national origin minority group parents of school activities which are called to the attention of other parents. Such notice in order to be adequate may have to be provided in a language other than English.

—from *The Federal Register* 35, 11595

The memorandum expanded the Civil Rights Act to prohibit discrimination based on language and cultural differences. Conventional practices, especially the use of standardized exam scores to place students in low ability or special education classes, were prohibited when they brought about the segregation of ethnic minority students. In effect, the 1973 *Lau* v. *Nichols* decision recognized the constitutionality of the memorandum when it ruled:

> It seems obvious that the Chinese-speaking minority receives fewer benefits than the English-speaking majority from respondents' school system which denies them a meaningful opportunity to participate in the educational program—all earmarks of the discrimination banned by the regulations . . . HEW issued. . . .

From *Brown* to *Lau*, the intentions of civil rights laws for schools have been to eradicate racism and ethnocentrism. Racism or ethnocentrism in the public schools are policies, programs, or practices that perpetuate the superiority of the majority WASP group over minority groups.

The next chapter provides an analysis of school policies, programs, and practices to demonstrate how they can be discriminatory.

Analysis of School Policy

School policy is stated in guidelines that enumerate the school rules but do not elucidate the assumptions upon which the rules are based. For example, a midwestern urban high school's grading policy reads in part: "teachers should compensate in their instruction and grading for the cultural deficiencies of the school's disadvantaged students."

This policy is based on potentially divisive assumptions: 1) Minority students aren't capable of the same high standards as majority group students; 2) minority students should be treated preferentially, since they have deficiencies; 3) minority students are culturally deficient rather than just different. These assumptions can disrupt multiethnic harmony, because they encourage preferential treatment of one group of students to the detriment of another, and they can cause both groups to realize less than their full potential. Student reaction might be: "Why work harder? The blacks get Bs and they don't do as much as we." Or, "No use to work harder anyway. The teacher doesn't think we [blacks] are very smart."

One way to monitor policies within a school is to form a human rights committee representing the administration, faculty, students, and supportive staff. The committee would maintain constant surveillance over policies and their effects when implemented. It would investigate complaints, conduct hearings, and mediate disputes among complainants. To insure due process, the committee would have the power to arbitrate human rights grievances. For example, if a group of Chicano students complain that more Chicanos than Anglos are suspended from their school, the committee should examine all the facts of the complaint. The facts may show that teachers have a double standard that is discriminatory against Chicanos. The teachers may enforce discipline rules more harshly with Chicanos than with Anglos. Thereby, the double standard causes Chicanos to be suspended more often than Anglo students. If the student body were one-fifth Chicanos, and if a much higher percentage of Chicanos were suspended than Anglo students, the committee might infer that a double standard exists and recommend several options to the principal to remedy the situation. Or it might find that Chicanos were breaking the rules more frequently than Anglos. If the Chicano students are not satisfied with the committee's action, they can request that the committee arbitrate the complaint. If the committee should again find that the teachers operated on a double standard, they would have the power to order the principal to remedy the situation.

The human rights committee could not arbitrate serious substantive policy grievances. In the above example, if the Chicano students complained that the suspension policy was inherently discriminatory and should be abolished, then the committee would have to refer the complaint to the school board. Because it is the school board's responsibility to determine policy, it would be responsible for abrogating a particular policy; it would also be responsible for conducting a fair hearing for the students' grievances. Thus, adoption of a human rights committee would cause a fundamental change in a school's governance structure. It would diffuse some of the administration's power, but it could also provide a more equitable implementation of policy.

Another way to monitor policy is to hire an ombudsman. The ombudsman, like a public defender, would investigate student complaints against the school. As with the human rights committee, the ombudsman would act in accordance with the facts of the complaint. Schools that can't afford to hire an ombudsman may give a teacher or counselor released time to act as an ombudsman. While a part-time ombudsman is less expensive, such an individual might experience a conflict of interest as a member of the school staff involved in the complaint. Perhaps a retired lawyer or superintendent could be persuaded to volunteer time to be an ombudsman. No doubt such persons would reflect mature judgment as well as save the school money. Still another way to monitor policy is to establish a human rights committee within every class. Then, as grievances arise, the teacher can charge the committee to assist in resolving the grievance.

Whatever policy-monitoring format is used, i.e., an ombudsman or a schoolwide or in-class human rights committee, the important consideration is the spirit in which the format is instituted and maintained. If a human rights committee is eyewash to appease students, then it serves no productive educative purpose. Indeed, it makes a mockery of democracy, teaching students that adults have little respect for democratic procedures and that human rights are not really important.

Analysis of Teaching and Supportive Staff Practices

Transmission of the culture is essential to teaching. The teacher transmits the culture through attitudes, beliefs, perceptions, language styles, and other personal attributes. Much of the transmission is unconscious. Many times teachers and other school personnel reveal their ethnic and social class biases through their routine practices. Native American students from Bureau of Indian Affairs boarding schools have told me of practices they perceived as racist. According to one account, whenever a Comanche student was heard speaking in the Comanche dialect, the teacher (or any other staff member) would hit the student to "beat the Comanche" out of him. Other native American students have told of having their hair cut by a school principal or of being forced to wear shoes on certain native American religious days in violation of tribal traditions.

Analysis of practices requires sensitivity to the pervading school climate. The school does not exist in a vacuum. As an integral part of the neighborhood, the local community, and the state, the school's climate will reflect the community. Teachers and staff serve as conduits through which the social climate is transmitted to the students in the school. Consequently, analysis of practices should focus on 1) the non-verbal and verbal behavior of the teachers and staff, 2) the intergroup relations and overall climate fostered in the school, and 3) the roles and responsibilities delegated to the students in the school.

Subtle practices that hinder multi-ethnic harmony may be discernible in the roles and responsibilities delegated to students. Which stu-

81676

dents traditionally receive most of the social rewards of the school? Do the minority students receive their fair share of the social rewards? Are they cheerleaders? Are they on the debate team? Who is involved in school plays? Which students are traditionally assigned to leadership duties in the school? Do members of the minority student groups escort school guests and visitors? Are members of the majority group always placed in charge of minority students?

Subtle manifestations of ethnic conflict can be discerned in the school's intergroup relations. When a fight occurs, is a sincere attempt made to determine whether the fight was caused by interpersonal or intergroup conflict? If the cause of the fight seems to derive from inter-group conflict, what is done to resolve the conflict and improve the interaction between the conflicting groups?

Tracking and ability grouping practices have a negative influence on the school's intergroup relations because these practices tend to iso-late students along cultural, racial, or economic lines and thereby per-petuate in-school segregation and unequal educational opportunity.

Ability grouping has the effect of segregating minority students within the school and dooming them to failure. Once placed in a low track, they rarely advance to a higher track. These students are deprived of the academic experiences and skills that would prepare them for col-lege entrance and a consequent professional career.

Also, tracking and ability grouping deprive majority students of positive relationships with minority students. Indeed, majority stu-dents develop a false sense of academic superiority. Tracking rein-forces that feeling of superiority and teaches the myth that the ma-jority group is superior to the minority groups. Under these circum-stances, what kind of positive attitudes toward minorities can the stu-dents learn?

The negative consequences of tracking and ability grouping—stereotyped attitudes toward minorities and predetermined academic failure for minority students—far outweigh whatever administrative expediencies tracking and ability grouping practices obtain. Both tracking and ability grouping should be abandoned and replaced by heterogeneous grouping or individualized instruction.

Counseling minority students into programs based on a single-interest inventory instrument or a culturally biased achievement test, or on stereotypic career aspirations and expectations, will tend to relegate those students to vocational programs. These types of counseling practices, compounded by tracking and ability grouping, are clearly discriminatory and are damaging to majority and minority students alike.

The verbal and nonverbal behavior of teachers and staff are important. I have visited teacher lounges where pejorative words such as "spooks" or "polacks" were used by teachers when referring to black and Polish students. Studies of the verbal and nonverbal communication patterns of some teachers indicate both a verbal and nonverbal bias against minority students. Nonverbal behavior includes the way the teacher manages the classroom, the congruence or incongruence between what the teacher says and implies, and the kind of body space relations established between the teacher and students.

Let me relate a personal experience to illustrate how bias can occur. A teacher invited me to visit his seventh-grade classroom to note the seating arrangement that purportedly accommodated both fast and slow learners. Some students sat in small groups throughout the center of the room, where they were to help each other. Other students sat alone facing the wall away from the center groups. According to the teacher, these students were slow learners, easily distracted, and needed the discipline imposed by this seating arrangement. They were not to talk or share information. All of the students facing the walls were black; the students in the small groups were white. Though the teacher denied he segregated students according to race, this permanent seating arrangement had the effect of racial segregation.

The teacher said that the "black kids are bused in from a poor neighborhood that has bad schools, so it takes them a while to catch up." Why couldn't the faster students help the slower students? Were the blacks really slower? Or were they labeled "slow learners" because of culturally biased test scores? These questions were not satisfactorily answered by the teacher, who incidentally, has never invited me back to his classroom. Nevertheless, the teacher's practice of isolating students according to race conveyed to the students notions of white superiority and black inferiority, a classic instance of nonverbal racism.

The above comments on teacher practices are equally applicable to the nonteaching staff, whose pervasive effect upon school climate should not be ignored. The attitude that a cafeteria worker, for example, takes toward certain ethnic foods will be communicated to students. If the cafeteria worker abhors bagels, then the abhorrence will be conveyed to both the Jewish and non-Jewish students. When I taught school in Wisconsin, I knew of a janitor who watched Polish students carefully when they went to the restroom because, according to him, "Polacks are known for their dirt," and they allegedly threatened the sanitary conditions of the restrooms. I could never figure out how the janitor could tell the difference between a Polish and non-Polish student!

Analysis of Curriculum Content

Curriculum content is the subject matter used in programs of instruction, e.g., math, science, language arts, the social studies, etc. Analysis of curriculum content requires a critical examination of the substance and process conveyed by the content. Multi-ethnic themes and concepts should permeate the content. It is not enough simply to add ethnic studies courses or units to an already crowded secondary social studies program, nor is it satisfactory to include a few minor characters to represent minority people in children's literature at the elementary school level. The additive approach—adding a few token units on minority historical events or cultural contributions—perpetuates the notion that minorities are not an integral part of society. Content analysis requires an examination of two questions directed at the ethnic characteristics of all curriculum content: 1) Is the content permeated with multi-ethnic themes and concepts? 2) What types of images are evoked by these themes and concepts?

Content should be viewed as a process that evokes images of people and groups. What image of Chinese Americans is evoked when teachers fail to discuss the economic impact of Chinese Americans on the development of the western U.S.? If students learn nothing about the courage, resourcefulness, and the endurance of the early Chinese Americans, then they must rely on stereotypic images learned outside of school. Chinese American students may internalize the image as appropriate for their self-concepts and adapt their classroom behavior to fit the stereotype.

Not only should the content of such subjects as the language arts, social studies, science, and math be examined for multi-ethnic themes and concepts, but the content of other subjects should be examined because they also operate on cultural assumptions. For example, what about the content in home economics? Is it permeated with multi-ethnic themes and concepts? Are the foods of minority groups studied from the perspective of dietary and nutritional value? In family and child development lessons, what kinds of family structures and relations are studied? Are such structures as the extended or single-parent family studied in terms of their ethnic and economic context? If these questions can't be answered with yes, then the curriculum cannot prepare students to live harmoniously in a multi-ethnic society.

The content of all subjects should be based on assumptions that convey multi-ethnic themes and concepts that evoke accurate images of U.S. society. The study of foreign cultures, while they are important links to U.S. ethnic groups, should not preclude the study of the history and status of the ethnic group cultures in the U.S. today. A lesson on Japan is no more synonymous with a study of the Japanese American experience than a lesson on Renaissance art is with the Italian American experience.

Three effective approaches have emerged for multi-ethnic education: 1) human rights, 2) intergroup relations, and 3) ethnic studies.

Human Rights Approach

The challenge of the human rights approach is to balance the civil rights of the group, e.g., senior class, homeroom, with the human rights of the student. The teacher must balance "law" with "order." The human right to be oneself may conflict with the group's civil right to an equal educational opportunity if one student insists on rolling drum sticks on a table during study sessions, for example.

The teacher determines which rights are to prevail at a given time. The teacher may want to involve the whole class in making the decision. For example, in the following classroom incident the teacher must decide between the group's right and the student's: The students in the third-grade class were working in small groups. Each group was cutting pictures from old magazines, when in one group Toby exclaimed, "Heck! Cutting pictures from magazines is sissy-stuff! I won't do it! And I won't give any of you the scissors to *cut your paper dolls!*"

Whose rights should prevail? The group's right to continue the project? Toby's right to be different? Should the teacher involve the group in making the decision?

One solution would be to explain to Toby that he has a right to be different but a concurrent responsibility to respect the rights of the others who may want to continue the project. Then Toby, the teacher, or the group, or any combination of the three could identify a task for Toby that would not violate his right while keeping him involved with the group.

What's important about the human rights approach is how the teacher handles conflicts of rights, because it is more difficult to practice respect for human rights than it is to merely advocate them. For example, in the case of a fire in a classroom, the teacher should take complete control of the group, insist on total conformity, and abrogate anyone's right to be different so that the group can be led out of the room to safety. But in the case of a student who is accused by the class of stealing the teacher's grade book, the teacher is challenged to handle the potential violation of rights with discretion so as to foster respect for the rights of the accused, i.e., the right of innocence until proved guilty, or the right to face one's accuser. The teacher's approach has to be situational, assessing carefully the incident and then deciding upon an approach that would protect the rights of the students.

Overall, the teacher is challenged to balance the group's and individual's rights in such a manner that a climate of respect for the rights of everyone predominates in the classroom. Assumptions of the human rights approach are:

Human rights are basic to a democratic society.
Students must know what their rights are before they can practice them.
Human rights must be valued in a democratic society.
Majority rules should not destroy individual student rights.
Students have the right to be different.
Students have the right to a positive self-concept.
Students can learn to use their rights responsibly.

The human rights approach stresses the importance of the inherent, human rights of teachers and students. Also stressed is the natural rights notion; i.e., humans have certain rights because they are human. These rights cannot be earned, deserved, or granted by a political body. They are presumed universal values expressed in the Declaration of Independence, the Magna Carta, and other moral codes.

Phi Delta Kappa's Teacher Education Project on Human Rights is an exemplary human rights program. The preamble to the program follows:

THE HUMAN RIGHTS CREED IN EDUCATION
Preamble

As an educator in a democratic society, concerned with the human rights of people everywhere, I will exemplify in my behavior a commitment to these rights. Educators and the educative process must have a more significant impact in insuring these rights for all people. Thus I will translate my belief in basic human rights into daily practice. I believe in the right and its concomitant responsibility:

1. To Equal Opportunity for All in:
   Education
   Housing
   Employment
   The Exercise of the Franchise
      and Representation in Government
2. Of Due Process and Equal Protection Under the Law
3. Of Freedom of Speech and of the Press
4. To Dissent
5. To Freedom of or from Religion
6. To Privacy
7. To Be Different
8. Of Freedom from Self-Incrimination
9. To a Trial by a Jury of Actual Peers
10. To Security of Person and Property
11. To Petition and Redress of Grievances
12. To Freedom of Assembly

Developed by Phi Delta Kappa
Commission on Education and Human Rights

Intergroup Relations Approach

A Native American prayer expresses the spirit of the intergroup relations approach:

> Grant that I may not criticize my neighbor until I have walked for a moon in his moccasins.

The purpose of intergroup relations is to teach students how to understand the feelings, beliefs, and perceptions of others. When students can genuinely empathize with each other, when they can genuinely walk in their neighbor's moccasins, they can begin to accept others and themselves as inherently worthy of respect, dignity, and integrity.

Compared to the human rights model that focuses on the teacher's governance techniques, the intergroup relations approach focuses on the affective relationships the teacher can nurture among students. Basic to the intergroup relations approach are these assumptions:

1. Man belongs to one biological family.
2. All groups have similarities and differences.
3. No group is innately superior to another.
4. Some groups are under restrictive social controls.

Schools that have no ethnic minority students can utilize simulations of cross-ethnic or cross-racial experiences. Many of you will remember the "brown eyes—blue eyes" experiment conducted by the Iowa school teacher. Jane Eliot wanted to teach her students *how it feels* to experience racial discrimination. Since she had no black students or adults to explain the experience, she got the class to discriminate against each other on the basis of eye color. One day the brown-eyed students were discriminated against in every way, except, of course, violence. The next day the blue-eyed students became the minority group and were discriminated against. At the end of the two days, all the students reported a deep sense of rage. They felt superior when discriminating and inferior when discriminated against. None was comfortable as either the oppressed or the oppressor. They learned the devastating nature of racism.

The challenge of the intergroup relations approach is to change elitist, ethnocentric, or racist attitudes. The teacher needs to manage the class so that students will have ample opportunities to learn the commonalities among groups without denigrating or ignoring the group differences.

The intergroup relations approach requires a socially sensitive teacher who understands students, the classroom social climate, and the way students feel about their ethnic or racial identity. Also, the teacher must be aware of the ethnic, racial, and social class relationships that exist in the community, especially since the same relationships may be paralleled in the school.

I am familiar with a high school that was troubled by gang fights among white students. A careful analysis of the community's racial and social class relations showed that one group of white students was from poor white homes, and the other groups were from affluent homes. Also, the parents of the white affluent students associated with an affluent group of black citizens. The white affluent citizens resented the poor white group because they feared that it would disrupt the relationship between the affluent black and white parents. The parental resentment was conveyed to students. The affluent whites vented their resentment by provoking fights among the poor white students. The poor white students defended themselves.

The intergroup relations approach is not easy, but techniques for fostering positive intergroup relations are available:

1. Students can study and discuss their ethnic heritage.
2. Ethnic minority group parents can be invited to school to visit and talk with students.
3. Students can study the contributions that all ethnic groups have made to the community.
4. Students can conduct surveys of their own ethnic group's geographic distribution and develop charts to record the information.
5. Students can make a multi-ethnic map of U.S. society using pictures from old magazines.
6. Any special ability of ethnic minority students, such as bilingualism, may be used to build their sense of belonging to the class. Sharing folktales, ethnic games, or songs are examples.
7. Playground activities can be monitored so that students practice cooperation and fair play.

8. Field trips to other schools with diverse student populations can be planned so that students of different ethnic backgrounds can have one-to-one cultural exchanges.

9. A multi-ethnic reading table or reading shelf can be maintained by the teacher and student. It might contain ethnic magazines, newspapers, and books, e.g., *Ebony, Jr., La Luz, Wee Wish Tree.*

10. Students and teachers may work with P.T.A. groups to conduct activities, such as a multi-ethnic song fest, that are cultural exchanges designed to improve community group relations.

11. A multi-ethnic student welcoming committee can be organized to greet all new students, teachers, and school personnel.

12. Role playing can be used to help students learn to take the role of out-groups as well as in-groups.

13. A multi-ethnic bulletin board can be maintained by the students to display reports, pictures, and other items about persons from various ethnic groups.

14. Students can work out a code covering sports, games, elections, and classroom behavior in which all students are treated as equals.

15. Students and teachers can discuss frankly instances in which name-calling, prejudice, or discrimination are practiced by students or teachers.

16. A teacher can use an intergroup incident that occurs in the school or community for helping students acquire a sound perspective.

17. A science teacher might demonstrate the similarities of racial groups by studying blood samples of blacks, Asians, etc.

18. Teachers in all subject areas can make an effort to incorporate a study of ethnic groups as they relate to the curriculum, e.g., Chinese math discoveries, black scientists, and American inventions.

19. Schoolwide activities, Chicano dramas, blues festivals, and dances should be planned and conducted to offer students positive multi-ethnic experiences.

20. Students should not be encouraged to develop fraternities, sororities, clubs, or cliques that would divide students along racial, ethnic, or socioeconomic lines. Instead, multi-ethnic clubs should be encouraged.

Teachers, administrators, and school board members should make attempts to develop positive multi-ethnic relationships in their communities. In particular, administrative officers can take charge of multi-ethnic community relations. School leaders can become familiar with ethnic group organizations, such as the Anti-Defamation League, LULAC (League of United Latin American Citizens), or the Urban League. These groups can be invited to the school to present their programs to the students and their parents. School leaders can develop positive relationships between school and community. They should provide assistance for efforts to improve housing conditions, recreational facilities, fair employment practices, and adult education within the community.

The school itself can become a community service center where buildings and facilities are available for vocational, civic, and recreational activities of the community. As such, the school can be used to bring the diverse ethnic groups together to share interests, perspectives, and aspirations. *Together, the people can build a sense of community, develop multi-ethnic relationships, and most important, develop friends across ethnic lines.* The school would then become a model of harmonious adult multi-ethnic intergroup relations.

Ethnic Studies Approach

The ethnic studies approach asserts that the best way to counter prejudices and stereotypes is by countering the ignorance that causes them. Ethnic group prejudices can be lessened with knowledge about a group's history, culture, and experience.

While the intergroup relations approach attempts to change the student's attitudes through cross-cultural experiences, the ethnic studies model attempts the same changes through educating students about ethnic groups. Basic concepts of the ethnic studies approach are:

1. A positive self-concept is possible with knowledge of one's ethnic group history, culture, and experience.

2. A positive attitude toward other ethnic groups is possible with knowledge of the group's history, culture, and experience.

3. Ethnic group prejudices and stereotypes can be lessened with knowledge about a group's history, culture, and experience.

Again, the basic assumption is that new data will change the student's prejudicial attitudes. For example, once he knows the significant role that Japanese Americans played in the agricultural development of the western states, a student will be less inclined to think of Japanese Americans in traditional stereotypes.

Ethnic studies specialist James Banks states that the fundamental purpose of ethnic studies is ethnic literacy, i.e., a profound understanding of the ethnic experience in U.S. society. He takes the position that school reform requires that multi-ethnic experiences permeate the entire school environment, and that one of the major goals of schools should be to create total school pluralism. To accomplish this goal, the ethnic studies approach should not be confined to the social studies or language arts programs, but instead should be diffused throughout the entire school program.

Banks was the chairman of a group of educators who developed multi-ethnic curriculum guidelines for the National Council for the Social Studies. The guidelines define philosophy, rationale, and specific approaches and techniques for schools to develop a multi-ethnic curriculum. The guidelines are based on the ethnic studies approach. They are cited in the resource section of this fastback.

Another ethnic studies specialist, Carlos Cortes, developed a conceptual model for teaching the Chicano experience. Although the model focuses on Chicanos, its concepts are applicable to the study of any ethnic minority group. Substitute Chicano for black or Asian or Indian and the paradigm would remain relevant.

Cortes's model proposes global frames of references requiring the study of ethnic groups in relation to 1) the development of North American civilization, 2) comparative and contrastive ethnic experiences, 3) the cultural richness and diversity of ethnic groups, 4) the organic, activist nature of ethnic groups, and 5) the humanity of ethnic groups.

Bilingual-bicultural education programs utilize the ethnic studies model to the degree that they teach the culture associated with the student's non-English native language. Teaching bilingually, i.e., using two languages as mediums of instruction, is not essentially different from teaching in one language. Using two languages and teaching about two cultures, one of them being the student's home culture, is bi-bilingual-bicultural instruction. This type of instruction requires use of the ethnic studies approach. More details on bilingual education are available in Phi Delta Kappa's fastback 84, *Learning in Two Languages* (also available in Spanish as fastback 84S).

Sometimes our best teaching resources are within our communities. A study of the local community would go far to explain the personal sacrifices and hardships its people have endured and accomplishments they have made. Invite a grandfather or grandmother to tell of the immigrant experience, or of the Jim Crow laws in the South; write a biography on a family who migrated from Oklahoma where blacks, American Indians, and whites once competed in rodeos; visit the local cemeteries where Saminskis and Radovichs are buried, but where Catholics, or Jews, or Protestants, or blacks, or Chicanos may be excluded. Church socials, mutual aid societies (e.g. Sons of Italy or G. I. Forum), archives in newspaper offices, and railroad and bus stations are all community resources useful for a study of local ethnic history.

Textbooks used for the multi-ethnic approach need to be examined for slights against ethnic minority groups. Half truths, racist myths, and omissions need to be identified. The essential question is, How are ethnic minorities treated in the textbooks? Are they treated in their own right? Or, are they treated only in relationship to WASP culture?

Scales and rating sheets developed to detect racist or ethnocentric biases in textbooks require the skill to infer the underlying, sometimes subtle, implications of a picture, story, or passage in a textbook. General questions such as, "Does the book contain only stereotypic images of black Americans?" presupposes a knowledge of black stereotypes. Quantitative questions such as, "How many times are blacks portrayed in leadership positions?" provide data from which reliable inferences can be drawn.

Human rights, intergroup relations, and ethnic studies are valid educational approaches. They attempt to change negative, racist, or ethnocentric attitudes through positive experiences and new data. The approaches have in common an abiding respect for individual dignity and worth.

Multi-Ethnic Policies and Programs

Although multi-ethnic education is a relatively new thrust, federal policy and monies as well as endorsements of professional education organizations continue to strengthen the movement. Federal policy regarding multi-ethnic education is enumerated in Title IX of the Elementary and Secondary Education Act (ESEA) as the "Ethnic Heritage Program."

Public and private nonprofit institutions, agencies, and organizations are eligible for funding under Title IX for planning, developing, establishing, or operating ethnic heritage programs. Programs funded under Title IX can 1) develop curriculum materials for use in elementary or secondary schools or in institutions of higher education relating to the history, geography, society, economy, literature, art, music, drama, language, and general culture of the group or groups with which the program is concerned, and the contributions of that ethnic group or groups to the American heritage; 2) disseminate curriculum materials to permit their use in elementary and secondary schools or institutions of higher education throughout the nation; 3) provide training for persons using, or preparing to use, multi-ethnic curriculum materials; 4) cooperate with persons and organizations with a special interest in the ethnic group or groups with which the program is concerned to assist them in promoting, encouraging, developing, or producing programs or other activities which relate to the history, culture, or traditions of that ethnic group or groups.

During 1976-77, 45 grants were made to public and private non-

40

profit education institutions, agencies, and organizations. Approximately 40% of the grants supported training projects, 40% supported multi-ethnic curriculum materials development, and 20% supported dissemination programs.

The American Association of Colleges for Teacher Education (AACTE) has endorsed multi-ethnic teacher education. Its policy, "No One Model American," reads in part:

> Multicultural education is education which values cultural pluralism. Multicultural education rejects the view that schools should seek to melt away cultural differences or the view that schools should merely tolerate cultural pluralism. To endorse cultural pluralism is to endorse the principle that there is no one model American. To endorse cultural pluralism is to understand and appreciate the differences that exist among the nation's citizens. It is to see these differences as a positive force in the continuing development of a society which professes a wholesome respect for the intrinsic worth of every individual.

The policy essentially endorses multi-ethnic teacher education for most, if not all, colleges and schools of education. Further, the AACTE is working jointly with the National Council for Accreditation of Teacher Education (NCATE) to formulate multi-ethnic teacher education standards. The new standards would require practically every college or school of education in the U.S. to provide multi-ethnic courses or experiences for education students, if those colleges and schools of education want to maintain NCATE accreditation.

Several critical multi-ethnic documents exist. The National Council for the Social Studies (NCSS) developed and disseminated *Curriculum Guidelines for Multiethnic Education*. The guidelines set policy, philosophy, rationale, and explicit guidelines for implementation of multi-ethnic education in public schools. The first guideline, and its subguidelines, set the curriculum guide's tone:

1.0 Does ethnic pluralism permeate the total school environment?

1.1 Is ethnic content incorporated into all aspects of the curriculum, preschool through grade 12 and beyond?

1.2 Do instructional materials treat ethnic differences and groups hon-

41

estly, realistically, and sensitively?

1.3 Do school libraries and resource centers have a variety of materials on the histories, experiences, and cultures of many different ethnic groups?

1.4 Do school assemblies, decorations, speakers, holidays, and heroes reflect ethnic group differences?

1.5 Are extracurricular activities multiracial and multi-ethnic?

The AACTE produced an analysis and annotated bibliography, *Multicultural Education and Ethnic Studies.* The document succinctly summarizes the philosophic history of multi-ethnic education and then provides a well-annotated bibliography on multi-ethnic books and materials.

Other professional organizations support multi-ethnic education. The National Council of Teachers of English (NCTE) published its policy on the student's right to speak a dialect. Basically, the policy, "The Student's Right to a Dialect," endorses linguistic pluralism by encouraging English and language arts teachers to respect the student's ethnic, social, or racial dialect. Also, NCTE publishes multi-ethnic articles and periodicals and fosters publication of multi-ethnic literature. To broaden its scope as well as to eliminate implications of language ethnocentrism, NCTE changed the title of its elementary education journal, *Elementary English,* to *Language Arts.* Along this line, the International Reading Association promotes and publishes bilingual and multi-ethnic articles and monographs. The Association for Supervision and Curriculum Development (ASCD) publishes articles on multi-ethnic education.

Phi Delta Kappa publishes articles on multi-ethnic education in the *Phi Delta Kappan,* and it also has published two fastbacks (nos. 84 and 87) and a book, *The Melting of the Ethnics: Education of the Immigrants,* on multi-ethnic concerns. The National Education Association endorsed bilingual-bicultural education as early as 1965, when it sponsored the first U.S. conference on bilingual-bicultural education. Other public and private organizations and agencies have endorsed or supported multi-ethnic education. The organizations that have the longest history of ongoing multi-ethnic developments are the Anti-Defamation League of B'nai B'rith and the National Council of Christians and Jews. Without a doubt, the Anti-Defamation League publishes some of the best curriculum resources and materials focused on multi-ethnic concerns. Of course, the grandfathers of the psychology of racism and ethnocentrism are Gordon Allport and Kenneth Clark. Allport is best known for his classic study of prejudice and discrimination, *The Nature of Prejudice*. Clark is best known for his work on the effects of racism and ethnocentrism on the self-concepts of black children.

The future of multi-ethnic education is bright. Resources, curriculum materials, and instructional programs are developing. Educators, politicians, and other professionals are promoting multi-ethnic thrusts. If the leadership for multi-ethnic education continues to pursue its goals of human rights and social harmony, and if programs are developed prudently, multi-ethnic education should continue to grow.

Myths and Realities

These are myths and realities central to multi-ethnic education:

Myth: Multi-ethnic education creates divisiveness by emphasizing ethnic differences. We should be emphasizing commonalities among groups.

Reality: Commonalities cannot be recognized unless differences are acknowledged. For too long we have ignored ethnic differences; we have treated ethnic differences as bad characteristics and thereby have not recognized commonalities or differences in American society.

Myth: Multi-ethnic education would shatter the melting pot.

Reality: A genuine melting pot society—one that molds all of its ethnic groups into one greater society—has never existed in the U.S. Actually, this kind of society is an ideal that must be continually nurtured. When U.S. society truly interweaves the best of all of its cultures, it will be a melting pot society.

Myth: Multi-ethnic education would not build a harmonious society.

Reality: One reason U.S. society is not harmonious is that certain groups have been denied their cultural rights. Multi-ethnic education would restore those rights by emphasizing cultural equality and respect.

Myth: Multi-ethnic education detracts from the basics in public schools. Students should be taught to read, write, and compute.

Reality: Multi-ethnic education need not detract from the basics of education. Students can be taught basic skills while also learning to respect cultures. A strong argument can be made for multi-ethnic education as a basic in education.

Myth: Multi-ethnic education is to enhance the self-concepts of ethnic minority students.

Reality: A half-true myth. Multi-ethnic education should enhance the self-concepts of all students because it provides a more balanced view of American society.

Myth: Multi-ethnic education is just a euphemism for "disadvantaged education."

Reality: Sociologists now believe that most American students are disadvantaged. Students living in suburban enclaves are far removed from the realities of American life. Some students in rural and inner-city enclaves experience second-rate classroom facilities and instruction. Multi-ethnic education would improve conditions for all students because it deals with the realities of American society and requires a superior type of instruction.

Myth: Teaching ethnic pride, such as black pride or Chicano pride, would also teach ethnic minority students to dislike white culture and students.

Reality: Pride is the wrong word. Teaching ethnic respect, respect for oneself and one's group, would cause the opposite reaction. To engender respect, a student must learn to respect others.

Myth: Our society has more fundamental problems, such as pollution, that should be countered by the schools.

Reality: One of our most serious cultural problems in American society is depletion of resources. Not only have we plundered our natural resources, we also have not developed our human resources. The ecological insights of native Americans and the bilingualism of the Spanish-speaking are only two examples of undeveloped human resources.

Myth: We now have laws that prohibit every conceivable form of ethnic and racial discrimination. We also have multi-ethnic educational approaches to teach students to live harmoniously in a multi-ethnic society. We no longer need to worry about ethnocentrism and racism.

Reality: Laws and educational approaches do not always change attitudes. People change attitudes in themselves and others. We must make multi-ethnic harmony a way of life if we want students to do the same.

Laws are not enough. People are harder to change than laws. Social justice requires fundamental changes in the social structure, changes which can only be made by individuals in their personal relations, homes, jobs, and churches. Teachers can begin the arduous struggle to reconcile American myths and realities, but the struggle will succeed only if buffered by individual, attitudinal change and judicious enforcement of the law. Historian Henry Steele Commager has said, "Our immediate problem is twofold: as citizens to bring about changes in the moral standards and habits of society, and as educators to see that our schools prepare the young for the obligations of citizenship in a just society. This requires that the schools themselves be just."

Multi-ethnic education challenges educators to advocate actively those assumptions fundamental to a pluralistic society and to promote a climate that allows students to understand their ethnicity as well as the ethnicity of others. Inherent in that climate should be such human rights as the right to be different, the right to be oneself, the right to dissent—with their concurrent responsibilities—so students can learn how to manage and to live harmoniously in a multi-ethnic society.

Last, we must all be able to answer three questions intelligently and honestly if we wish to develop a harmonious, multi-ethnic society:

1. Do I know the meaning of race, nationality, ethnicity, and ethnic minority and majority groups and their significance in American society?

2. Do I accept or denigrate ethnic differences as factors in the American scene?

3. How am I resolving the American dilemma?

Multi-Ethnic Resources

Organizations that publish multi-ethnic teaching materials:

Asian American Studies Center
Box 24A43
Los Angeles, CA 94104
(Ethnic studies materials on the Asian American experience.)

Chicano Studies Center
University of California
405 Hilgard Avenue
Los Angeles, CA 90024
(Chicano ethnic studies material. Also publishes *Aztlan,* foremost research journal on Mexican Americans.)

Council on Interracial Books for Children
1841 Broadway
New York, NY 10023
(Critiques of children's literature on sexism and racism. The monthly *Bulletin* is filled with excellent multi-ethnic materials and resources.)

Indian Historical Society
1451 Masonic Avenue
San Francisco, CA 94117
(Native American curriculum materials. Good nonstereotypic children's literature about native Americans.)

Johnson Publishing Company
820 South Michigan Avenue
Chicago, IL 60605
(*Ebony, Jr.* and other materials on black Americans.)

Puerto Rican Research and Resource Center
1529 Connecticut Avenue, N.W.
Washington, DC 20036
(Good basic materials on Puerto Ricans.)

The Anti-Defamation League of B'nai B'rith
315 Lexington Avenue
New York, NY 10016
(Materials, films, filmstrips on racism, prejudice, stereotyping.)

Multi-ethnic Publications:

Banks, James. *Teaching Strategies for Ethnic Studies.* Boston, Mass.:
Allyn and Bacon, 1975.
Concepts, strategies, and materials for teaching about Asians,
blacks, Chicanos, Puerto Ricans, native Americans. Contains orig-
inal, well-researched data and an excellent multi-ethnic resource
unit.

Castañeda, Alfredo. *The Educational Needs of Minority Groups.*
Lincoln, Neb.: Professional Educators Publications, 1974.
Sociological analysis of the educational status and concerns of
blacks, Chicanos, and native Americans.

Cortes, Carlos. *Understanding You and Them: Tips for Teaching
About Ethnicity.* Boulder, Colo.: Social Science Consortium, 1976.
Basic information on ethnicity. A "how to" book with plenty of examples and suggestions for improving intergroup relations in
schools.

Garcia, Ricardo. *Learning in Two Languages.* Bloomington, Ind.:
Phi Delta Kappa, 1976.
A PDK fastback (No. 84) on bilingual-bicultural education. Avail-
able in English and Spanish.

Grambs, Jean D. *Intergroup Relations: Methods and Materials*. Engle-
wood Cliffs, N.J.: Prentice-Hall, 1968.
Basic concepts, assumptions, and methods for improving inter-
group relations in schools.
Guide for Improving Public School Practices in Human Rights.
Bloomington, Ind.: Phi Delta Kappa, 1975.
Information on human rights plus programs for teaching human
rights with administrators, teachers, and students. Evaluation ma-
terial on attitudes toward human rights, sexism, and racism in the
school curriculum. Excellent annotated bibliography.
Henderson, George. *Human Relations: From Theory to Practice*.
Norman, Okla.: University of Oklahoma Press, 1974.
Good basic discussion on practical aspects of human relations
studies.
Multiethnic Curriculum Guidelines. Washington, D.C.: National
Council for the Social Studies, 1976.
Philosophy, rationale, and guidelines for assessing school curric-
ulum for multi-ethnic experiences. Guidelines in narrative and
checklist formats.

Multi-ethnic Legislation and Policy:
"Ethnic Heritage Studies Program"
ESEA, Title IX
HEW, Office of Education
Ethnic Heritage Studies Branch
Washington, DC 20202

"No One Model American"
American Association of Colleges for Teacher Education
One Dupont Circle, N.W.
Washington, DC 20036

For state and local resources, contact your state department of education, in care of human relations or multicultural education. Also, contact the ethnic studies departments on college and university
campuses.